IXL SUMMER WORKBOOK

THE ULTIMATE SUMMER WORKBOOK

FOR THE SUMMER BETWEEN GRADES 1 & 2

© 2025 IXL Learning. All rights reserved. No part of this publication may be reproduced, stored in a retrieval system, or transmitted, in any form or by any means (electronic, mechanical, photocopying, recording, or otherwise) without the prior written permission of IXL Learning.

ISBN: 978-1-964670-04-1
29 28 27 26 25 1 2 3 4 5

Printed in the USA

About this book

Keep your child engaged with learning over summer break with the Ultimate IXL Summer Workbook! The activities in this workbook are perfect for reinforcing key skills from the past year and building new skills in preparation for the year ahead.

DAILY PRACTICE

This workbook contains <u>60 days</u> of activities. Each day consists of 2 full pages of activities that can be completed in about 15 minutes. At 5 days per week, this workbook is perfect for a 12-week summer break! Throughout the week, your child will engage in math and language arts activities, complete a science or social studies page, and wrap up with enrichment activities.

BRAIN BREAKS

Brain breaks are sprinkled throughout. These fun breaks include physical and sensory activities.

ACTIVITY TRACKER

Track your child's progress with the activity tracker! Have your child color in the bubble or cover it with a sticker after completing each day's work. Watch as the tracker fills up throughout the summer!

CERTIFICATE OF COMPLETION

Found at the back of the book, the certificate of completion is a great way to help you recognize your child's hard work!

Materials: To complete this workbook, your child will need a pencil, crayons or colored pencils, and a ruler.

Continue the fun with IXL.com!

Throughout the book, look for these IXL.com skill IDs. For additional practice, go to the website or the IXL mobile app and enter the three-digit code into the search bar.

IXL.com skill ID
ZUQ

IXL provides all the tools your child needs to succeed.

LIMITLESS LEARNING

Unlock your child's full potential with access to 17,000 engaging units in math, English, science, social studies, and Spanish. With examples and 1,300 video lessons across all grade levels, your learner can review a concept before diving into a skill.

PERSONALIZED PLAN

IXL's Diagnostic pinpoints your child's knowledge level and creates a customized plan to boost achievement.

REAL-TIME FEEDBACK

Detailed explanations after missed questions allow your child to learn from mistakes and work toward achieving mastery.

AWARDS AND CERTIFICATES

Whimsical awards and certificates help you celebrate your child and keep motivation high.

EDUCATIONAL GAMES

Fun-filled games provide hands-on practice in essential concepts and help your child develop a love of learning.

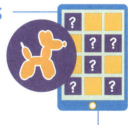

20% off For a limited time, receive 20% off your IXL family membership. Visit **www.ixl.com/workbook/12s** or scan the **QR code** for details.

© IXL Learning

Activity tracker

Keep track of your progress! Color in the bubble or cover it with a sticker after you complete each day's work.

Week 1
Days 1–5
1 2 3 4 5

Week 2
Days 6–10
6 7 8 9 10

Week 3
Days 11–15
11 12 13 14 15

Week 4
Days 16–20
16 17 18 19 20

Week 5
Days 21–25
21 22 23 24 25

Week 6
Days 26–30
26 27 28 29 30

Week 7
Days 31–35
31 32 33 34 35

Week 8
Days 36–40
36 37 38 39 40

Week 9
Days 41–45
41 42 43 44 45

Week 10
Days 46–50
46 47 48 49 50

Week 11
Days 51–55
51 52 53 54 55

Week 12
Days 56–60
56 57 58 59 60

© IXL Learning

Weeks 1–3: Overview

Week 1

Math
Addition and subtraction within 10
Number sequences

Language arts
Beginning and ending sounds
Reading for details
Plural nouns

Social studies
Using a map key

Enrichment
Shape sudoku
Spot the shadow

Week 2

Math
Addition within 20
Two-dimensional shapes

Language arts
Homophones
Nouns and verbs
Short vowel sounds

Science
Push and pull

Enrichment
Color to 100
Handwriting

Week 3

Math
Subtraction within 20
Equal parts

Language arts
Consonant blends
Story elements
Fact and opinion

Social studies
Land features

Enrichment
Logic puzzle
Imaginary animals

5
© IXL Learning

More ways to learn

Keep the learning going! Summer is the perfect time to explore, learn, and have fun. Use these simple, exciting activities to help you stay active, curious, and creative during your summer break.

See how many activities you can do! Cross off each activity as you complete it.

Build an obstacle course. 	Go outside and draw with sidewalk chalk. 	Complete a jigsaw puzzle. 
Play a card game with a friend. 	Plan the week's dinner menu. 	Learn a new jump rope trick. 
Learn the words of a new song. 	Make homemade ice cream with a family member. 	Build paper airplanes and have a race. 

DAY 1 — Add and subtract within 10

IXL.com skill ID **V7A**

Add or subtract.

4 + 2 = _____

1 + 9 = _____

3 − 0 = _____

3 + 2 = _____

2 − 2 = _____

2 + 6 = _____

10 − 1 = _____

0 + 2 = _____

8 − 4 = _____

9 − 8 = _____

7 − 2 = _____

5 + 4 = _____

3 + 3 = _____

4 − 3 = _____

8 + 1 = _____

5 − 4 = _____

7 + 3 = _____

9 − 3 = _____

3 + 4 = _____

10 − 7 = _____

Exclusive offer! For a limited time, receive 20% off your IXL family membership.

Scan the QR code or visit www.ixl.com/workbook/12s for details.

DAY 2 — Beginning and ending sounds

IXL.com skill ID **ZUQ**

Fill in the missing letters.

DAY 2 Use a map key

IXL.com skill ID
7VG

Maps use symbols to show where things are. The **map key** tells you what the symbols mean.

Use the map key to answer each question.

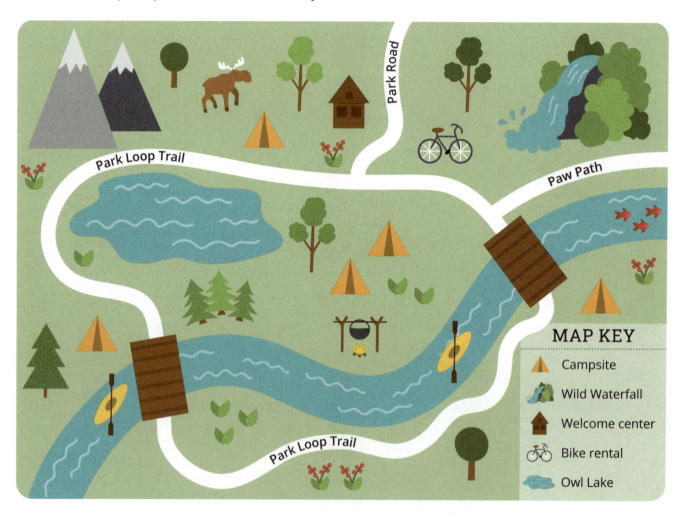

Find the welcome center on the map. What road is it near?

    Paw Path   Park Road

Find Wild Waterfall on the map. Is it closer to the bike rental or Owl Lake?

    Bike rental   Owl Lake

How many campsites are on the map? _____

DAY 3 — Reading for details

IXL.com skill ID **RYS**

Read the passage. Then use details from the passage to color the picture.

Seth and Devon share a room. Their carpet is gray. The table is made of brown wood. The brothers have green blankets on their beds.

Seth's bed is next to the window. He has orange pillows. Every day, he checks his plant on the shelf. The plant is in a red pot.

Devon has blue and yellow striped pillows on his bed. Yesterday, he put a yellow trophy on the bottom shelf next to the purple box.

Beep! The blue clock under the green lamp beeps. Time to start the day!

DAY 3 Add within 20

Fill in the blanks to add.

___7___ + ___4___ = ___11___

_____ + _____ = _____

_____ + _____ = _____

Add. Draw models to help.

7 + 7 = _____	3 + 10 = _____
4 + 8 = _____	8 + 9 = _____

12 © IXL Learning — MATH

DAY 4 Plural nouns

IXL.com skill ID
J9P

Fill in the blanks. Write the plural form of each noun.

We sleep in big yellow _____**tents**_____ when we camp.
tent

Grandpa bought two ice cream _____ for us.
cone

There are two _____ near Maple Falls.
lake

Our garden is full of pink _____.
flower

Many _____ buzz around the field.
bee

I saw two _____ at the zoo.
fox

My _____ splash in the pool.
sister

We fly _____ every year at the beach.
kite

Please clean the _____ after you paint.
brush

I love to eat fresh _____ all summer long.
peach

 **Brain Break!** Use your pointer finger to write your name or a message in the air.

DAY 4: Number sequences

IXL.com skill ID
ZBW

Write the missing numbers.

6	7			9	10	

17			19	20			22

48			50			52	

64	65				68	

79			81				84

96				99		

106			108			

		116			118		

14

© IXL Learning

MATH

DAY 5 Shape sudoku

Draw the shape to complete each row, column, and block. Each shape must appear only once in each row, column, and block. Be sure to use the right color!

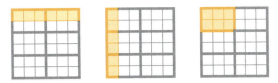

ENRICHMENT

DAY 5
Spot the shadow

Look at each object. Circle the shadow that matches.

DAY 6 Homophones

IXL.com skill ID
F6T

Circle the word that matches each picture.

Draw a picture to match each word.

aunt	ant

DAY 6: Add within 20

IXL.com skill ID: **6TM**

Add. Draw a line between the matching answers.

3 + 5 = 8   7 + 3

4 + 6   8 + 8

9 + 5   2 + 6 = 8

5 + 7   10 + 4

7 + 8   4 + 8

6 + 10   9 + 9

7 + 6   9 + 6

10 + 8   8 + 5

Boost your learning and save 20%. Join IXL today!

Scan this QR code for details.

DAY 7: Sentence order

The sentences in the stories below are in the wrong order. Write numbers to put the sentences in the correct order. Look for words like **first**, **next**, **then**, **after**, **later**, and **last** to help you.

__1__ Henry opened his birthday gifts.

__3__ After eating cake, we played tag outside.

__2__ Next, we ate birthday cake and ice cream.

____ After he finished the painting, he showed Papa.

____ Nick set up his paint supplies.

____ Then, Nick painted a colorful sunset.

____ When it is time for lunch, Rosa will help cook.

____ After they eat, they will clean up.

____ Today, Rosa is home with her dad.

____ Last, they will go to the park.

____ Then we went on a hike before dinner.

____ Last weekend, we went camping.

____ Later that night, we sang songs near the fire.

____ We unpacked and set up our tent right away.

DAY 7 Two-dimensional shapes

The corners of shapes can be called **vertices**. Write the number of vertices and sides in each shape.

Vertices: __4__

Sides: __4__

Vertices: _____

Sides: _____

Vertices: _____

Sides: _____

Vertices: _____

Sides: _____

Vertices: _____

Sides: _____

Vertices: _____

Sides: _____

Read about each shape. Then draw the shape and write its name.

This shape has 3 sides and 3 vertices.	This shape has 4 vertices and 4 sides of the same length.
Shape name: _____	Shape name: _____

DAY 8: Nouns and verbs

A **noun** names a person, animal, place, or thing. A **verb** tells you what a noun does.

Look at the bold word in each sentence. Is it a noun or a verb? Circle the answer.

Ella **runs** to Middle Hill Park every day.	noun	(verb)
Brooks walked home before dinner.	noun	verb
We **ate** lunch at the table outside.	noun	verb
Ava visits the **beach** with her family.	noun	verb
A green **frog** jumped into the pond.	noun	verb
Emma and Jack **dig** holes in the dirt.	noun	verb
It is a great day to fly my new **kite**!	noun	verb
Liz **finds** a shiny penny on the sidewalk.	noun	verb

Write a sentence about your family. Circle a noun and a verb.

_____

_____

 Can you exercise your face? Wiggle your eyebrows up and down as fast as you can. Try raising one eyebrow at a time!

LANGUAGE ARTS © IXL Learning 21

DAY 8 Push and pull

Forces can make things move. A **push** moves an object away from you. A **pull** moves an object toward you.

Each picture shows a push or a pull. Circle the answer.

push (pull)	push pull	push pull
push pull	push pull	push pull
push pull	push pull	push pull

DAY 9 — Add within 20

IXL.com skill ID **DF7**

Complete the puzzle.

Puzzle equations:
- ___ + 2 = 11
- 7 + 8 = ___
- ___ = 16
- ___ + 6 = ___
- ___ = 16
- 7 + ___ = ___
- 10 + ___ = 18
- ___ + ___ = 12
- 6 + ___ = 13
- 8 + ___ = 17
- 4 + ___ = ___

DAY 9 Short vowel words

Fill in the missing letters.

| f | a | n |

| w | | b |

| h | | l | l |

| | | t |

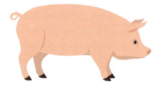

| p | | |

| f | | |

| | | |

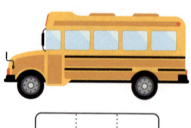

| | | |

| | | |

| | | |

| | | |

| | | |

DAY 10

Color to 100

Fill in the missing numbers to complete the hundreds chart. Then use the key to color the chart. What do you see?

GREEN	15, 16, 24, 25, 26, 27, 35, 36
ORANGE	45, 47, 54, 56, 58, 63, 65, 67, 74, 76, 78, 83, 85, 87, 94, 96
YELLOW	44, 46, 53, 55, 57, 64, 66, 68, 73, 75, 77, 84, 86, 88, 95, 97
BLUE	All numbers between 1 and 10. All numbers ending in 0, 1, 2, or 9. 13, 14, 17, 18, 23, 28, 33, 34, 37, 38, 43, 48, 93, 98

1	2	3				7	8		10
	12			15	16			19	
		23	24		26		28		30
31	32		34			37			40
41		43		45		47		49	
	52		54				58	59	
61				65	66		68		70
		73				77		79	
	82			85		87	88		
91		93	94						100

ENRICHMENT

25

© IXL Learning

DAY 10 Handwriting

Trace the sentences.

Elephants spend a lot
of time near water.
They love taking mud
baths!

Copy the sentences. Use your neatest handwriting!

DAY 11 — Consonant blends

Fill in the missing letters.

| c | l | u | b | | | a | g | | p | o | | |

| r | a | | | | b | o | | | | | i | n | g |

| | | i | c | k | | | e | s | s | | | o | c | k |

| | | u | | | | a | | | | a | |

DAY 11 Word problems

IXL.com skill ID **N5N**

Write an addition sentence to solve each problem.

Gabe puts 6 lemon cookies and 6 berry cookies on a plate. How many cookies are there in all?

_____ + _____ = _____ cookies

There are 5 boys and 8 girls in the Green Turtles swim class. How many total kids are in the Green Turtles swim class?

_____ + _____ = _____ kids

Carmen is at the beach. She finds 7 shells in the sand. Then she finds 4 more shells. How many shells does Carmen find?

_____ + _____ = _____ shells

There are 9 green apples and 7 red apples in a bowl. How many apples are in the bowl in all?

_____ + _____ = _____ apples

Helen picks some flowers for her aunt. She picks 3 red flowers and 9 pink flowers. How many flowers does Helen pick in all?

_____ + _____ = _____ flowers

DAY 12 Story elements

Read the passage. Then answer the questions.

Ari's Lake Walk

Ari smiled as she walked by the lake in her green shirt and new glasses. She wished she could stay there all day because there was so much to see!

The sun was bright in the sky. A flock of birds flew high above the water. Green trees stood tall around the lake. Some squirrels found nuts near the lake. A blue and yellow fish jumped out of the water with a splash. Ari loved watching the amazing animals all around her.

Who is the main character in the story? _____

Circle the picture that best shows the main character.

Draw a picture that shows the setting.

DAY 12: Subtract within 20

Fill in the blanks to subtract.

12 − 4 = 8

____ − ____ = ____

____ − ____ = ____

Subtract. Draw models to help.

9 − 2 = ____

12 − 9 = ____

11 − 5 = ____

14 − 7 = ____

DAY 13: Fact and opinion

IXL.com skill ID
79N

A **fact** is something that can be proved right or wrong.

An **opinion** is what a person believes, thinks, or feels.

Read each sentence. Write an F next to the facts.
Write an O next to the opinions.

__O__ Sweet corn tastes really good.	____ Apples are a type of fruit.
____ Water can turn into ice.	____ Summer is too hot.
____ A square has four sides.	____ Cookies are better than cake.
____ Swimming is fun.	____ Bees make honey.

Now you try! Write one fact and one opinion about summer.

Fact	
Opinion	

DAY 13 Equal parts

Circle each shape that is split into equal parts.

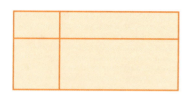  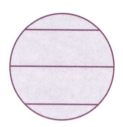

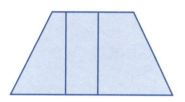  

 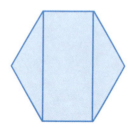 

Get ahead of the curve with extra practice! Join IXL today.

Scan this QR code or visit www.ixl.com/workbook/12s for details.

DAY 14 Pronouns

IXL.com
skill ID
MWM

A **pronoun** takes the place of a noun in a sentence.

Some of the most common pronouns are listed below:

| I | you | he | she | it | me |
| him | her | we | us | they | them |

Circle the pronouns in the sentences below.

(He) played in the pool with (them) for hours yesterday.

I gave her a birthday present.

She is taking us to the zoo this weekend.

Dad, can you read this book to me tonight?

We saw a show in the park, and it was a lot of fun!

He asked if they wanted to join him for a bike ride.

I think we should get them some popcorn, too.

Write about someone who makes you laugh. Use at least one pronoun. Circle the pronoun.

_____

_____

 **Brain Break!** | Take a look outside and watch the clouds. What shapes do you see?

DAY 14 Land features

Read about the land features below. Then label each land feature.

Land feature	About
hill	land that is a little higher than the other land around it
island	land with water on all sides
plain	flat land with few trees
valley	a low area of land between mountains or hills
mountain	land that rises high above the other land around it and is often steep
canyon	land with steep cliffs on both sides and often has a river running through it

valley

DAY 15

Imaginary animals

Time to get creative! Draw new animals based on the prompts.

An elephant with three trunks	A moose that can fly
A shark with four legs	A wolf that glows in the dark

ENRICHMENT

DAY 15 Logic puzzle

Sasha, Levi, and Jordan spend the day at the pool. Each friend brings a different pool float.

Which pool float does each friend bring? Use the clues and the grid to help you find out.

- Sasha does not bring the dinosaur float.
- Jordan's float is not shaped like an animal.
- Levi brings a green float with short arms.

		Pool float		
		Dinosaur	Flamingo	Donut
Friend	Sasha			
	Levi			
	Jordan			

Use your answers from the grid to finish the sentences.

Sasha brings the _____ float.

Levi brings the _____ float.

Jordan brings the _____ float.

36

© IXL Learning

ENRICHMENT

Weeks 4–6: Overview

Week 4

Math
Relate addition and subtraction
Subtraction within 20

Language arts
Double consonants and -ck
Subject-verb agreement
Fiction and reality

Science
Solids and liquids

Enrichment
Riddles
Finding pairs

Week 5

Math
Subtraction word problems
Picture graphs

Language arts
Synonyms
Consonant digraphs
Alphabetical order

Social studies
Jobs and tools

Enrichment
Number pattern maze
Crack the code

Week 6

Math
Addition and subtraction mixed practice
Adding three numbers

Language arts
Silent -e words
Real-life connections
Ending punctuation

Science
Weather and seasons

Enrichment
Sudoku
Drawing challenge

More ways to learn

Keep the learning going! Use these simple, exciting activities to help you stay active, curious, and creative during your summer break.

See how many activities you can do! Cross off each activity as you complete it.

Make a care package for someone special and send it to them. 	**Go for a hike or a nature walk.** 	**Try out a new recipe with a family member.** 
Learn how to say "hello" in another language. 	**Try out a new yoga pose.** 	**Create something new with an old cardboard box.** 
Put on your favorite song and dance around your room. 	**Read a book to a family member or stuffed animal.** 	**Start a new collection of objects, such as stamps or rocks.** 

DAY 16 — Relate addition and subtraction

IXL.com skill ID **DM2**

Fill in the missing number in each pair.

3 + 5 = __8__

__8__ − 3 = 5

10 − 6 = _____

6 + _____ = 10

12 − 2 = _____

2 + _____ = 12

8 + 8 = _____

_____ − 8 = 8

7 + 4 = _____

_____ − 7 = 4

13 − _____ = 5

_____ + 5 = 13

_____ + 10 = 15

15 − _____ = 10

_____ − 6 = 7

6 + 7 = _____

11 − _____ = 5

_____ + 5 = 11

_____ + 8 = 17

17 − _____ = 8

DAY 16 — Double consonants and -ck

IXL.com skill ID **R88**

Fill in the missing letters.

d o l l

r o _ _

b e _ _

b u _ _

g r a _ _

c l i _ _

t r _ _ _

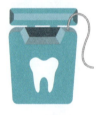
f l _ _ _

c r _ _ _

Write a sentence using two words from above.

_____

_____

40 © IXL Learning LANGUAGE ARTS

DAY 17 Solids and liquids

A **solid** has a shape of its own. A **liquid** takes the shape of its container.

Look at each picture. Then circle whether each item is a solid or a liquid.

lemonade	crayons	books
solid (liquid)	solid liquid	solid liquid
water in a pool	**olive oil**	**slide**
solid liquid	solid liquid	solid liquid
apple juice	**teddy bear**	**puddle**
solid liquid	solid liquid	solid liquid

SCIENCE

DAY 17: Subject-verb agreement

Read each subject and choose the correct verb. Find the path from start to finish.

DAY 18: Subtract within 20

IXL.com skill ID
PV5

Subtract. Draw a line between the matching answers.

7 − 2 = 5

12 − 6

14 − 10

16 − 8

12 − 9

18 − 9

15 − 5

14 − 7

9 − 5

10 − 7

15 − 9

13 − 4

14 − 6

12 − 5

13 − 8 = 5

19 − 9

Brain Break! Can you breathe like a bunny? Take three quick sniffs through your nose. Then, breathe out slowly through your nose.

Spelling

DAY 18

IXL.com skill ID **J86**

Use the letters in each word to spell a new word! Use the picture as a clue.

act	shoe	reap
cat		
inks	**nets**	**save**
melon	**heart**	**beard**
notes	**petal**	**skate**

44

© IXL Learning

LANGUAGE ARTS

DAY 19: Equal parts

Split each shape into 2 equal parts to make halves.

Split each shape into 3 equal parts to make thirds.

Split each shape into 4 equal parts to make fourths.

Exclusive offer!
For a limited time, receive 20% off when you join IXL today. Scan this QR code for details.

DAY 19 Fiction and reality

Which could happen in real life? Look at the pictures and circle the answers.

Read each pair of sentences. Put an X next to the sentence that could happen in real life.

____ We packed our things and moved to a new house.

____ Our house stood up and walked to a new town.

____ The scissors said, "Be careful! I am sharp!"

____ Bruno carefully used the scissors.

____ Laura's dog asked her to take a picture of him.

____ Laura took a picture of her dog playing.

DAY 20: What am I?

IXL.com skill ID **7QZ**

Circle the answer for each riddle.

I am sweet.
Bees make me.
People put me in tea.
What am I?

    milk   honey

I can be any color.
You might fold me.
You can write on me.
What am I?

    pen   paper

I am made from water and dirt.
You might find me after it rains.
I make your shoes dirty.
What am I?

    mud   garden

I might be on paper.
I could be on a phone.
I'll show you where to go.
What am I?

    lock   map   book

I am round like a cup.
Many times, I am in a tree.
I hold baby birds that chirp.
What am I?

    nut   plate   nest

You can hear me.
You can make me.
I might be loud or quiet.
What am I?

    sound   smell   taste

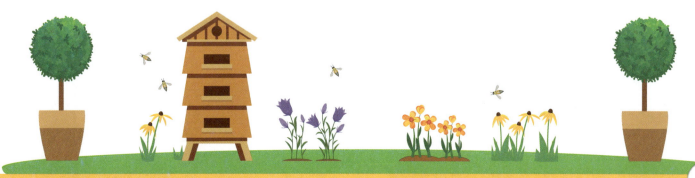

ENRICHMENT

DAY 20 Find the pairs

Find what doesn't belong! Draw lines to match the food truck pairs. Circle the food truck that does not have a match.

DAY 21 Synonyms

IXL.com skill ID
8NP

Synonyms are words with the same meaning or almost the same meaning.

Complete the crossword puzzle. Use the word bank to help you.

Word bank
- ~~press~~
- soft
- shiny
- toss
- repair
- start
- grin
- pal
- boat
- sound

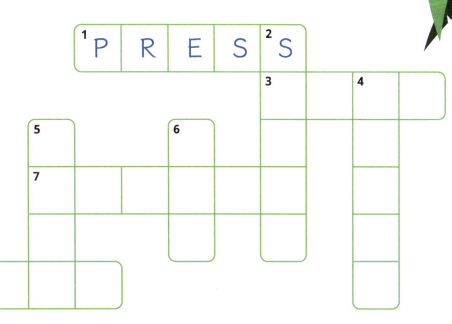

Across:
1. Synonym for **push**
   P R E S S
3. Synonym for **throw**
   ___ ___ ___ ___
7. Synonym for **fix**
   ___ ___ ___ ___ ___ ___
9. Synonym for **noise**
   ___ ___ ___ ___ ___
10. Synonym for **gentle**
    ___ ___ ___ ___

Down:
2. Synonym for **begin**
   ___ ___ ___ ___ ___
4. Synonym for **bright**
   ___ ___ ___ ___ ___
5. Synonym for **smile**
   ___ ___ ___ ___
6. Synonym for **friend**
   ___ ___ ___
8. Synonym for **ship**
   ___ ___ ___ ___

DAY 21 Subtract within 20

IXL.com skill ID
JJS

Find the path from start to finish. Follow the correct answers to the end.

START

9 − 3	5	7 − 3	3	10 − 2
6		6		8
11 − 2	9	15 − 8	7	13 − 4
8		8		9
18 − 9	6	12 − 3	7	14 − 7
9		9		8
17 − 9	6	16 − 10	7	11 − 6
8		8		6
18 − 8	10	14 − 5	9	FINISH

50 © IXL Learning   MATH

DAY 22 — Consonant digraphs

IXL.com skill ID **PN8**

Fill in the missing letters. Each pair of letters will be used more than once.

> ch   sh   th   ph   wh

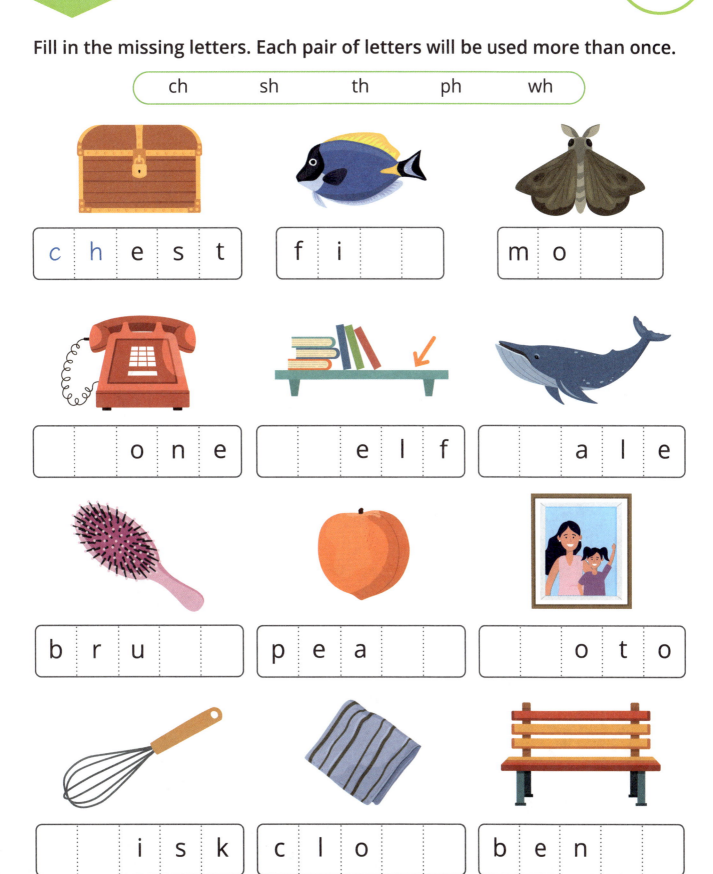

- c h e s t
- f i _ _
- m o _ _
- _ _ o n e
- _ _ e l f
- _ _ a l e
- b r u _ _
- p e a _ _
- _ _ o t o
- _ _ i s k
- c l o _ _
- b e n _ _

DAY 22 — Jobs and tools

Draw a line to match each job name with the correct tool.

artist

chef

carpenter

scientist

firefighter

hair stylist

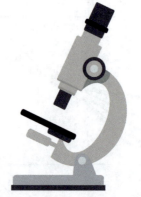

doctor

dentist

DAY 23 Word problems

Write a subtraction sentence to solve each problem.

Kelly sees 10 ducks in a pond. Then 5 of them fly away. How many ducks are left in the pond?

_____ – _____ = _____ ducks

Mr. Smith has 11 chickens on his farm. Mr. Hart has 9 chickens on his farm. How many more chickens does Mr. Smith have than Mr. Hart?

_____ – _____ = _____ more chickens

Maria has 12 eggs in a basket. She uses 4 of the eggs to make a cake. How many eggs are left over?

_____ – _____ = _____ eggs

Pete has 16 crayons. Maya has 6 crayons. How many more crayons does Pete have than Maya?

_____ – _____ = _____ more crayons

There are 13 kids at the park. Then 7 kids go home for dinner. How many kids are at the park now?

_____ – _____ = _____ kids

 Stand up and stretch your arms above your head. Reach as high as you can go!

DAY 23 Reading comprehension

IXL.com skill ID **2MH**

Read the passage. Then answer the questions.

Collecting Stickers and Coins

Do you like collecting things? When you **collect**, you gather one kind of thing. You might like collecting stickers or coins.

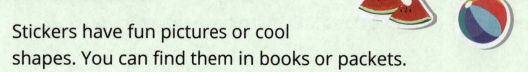

Stickers have fun pictures or cool shapes. You can find them in books or packets.

Coins can come from all over the world. They may have pictures of special places or people.

Collecting can take time. Start with a few stickers or coins, and collect more little by little. What would you like to collect?

What is this passage mostly about? Put an X next to the correct answer.

____ collecting toys   ____ collecting stickers and coins   ____ collecting dolls

The word **collect** means _____

_____.

Coins might have pictures of special _____ or _____.

What do you like to collect? _____

_____

DAY 24: Picture graphs

IXL.com skill ID
NM5

Jay is at the park with lots of other kids. He makes a tally chart of where the kids are playing.

Place	Number of kids
Swings	||||
Splash pad	⁄⁄⁄⁄⁄ |||
Slide	||
Sandbox	⁄⁄⁄⁄⁄ |

Use the tally chart to complete the picture graph.

Where kids are playing at the park	
Swings	☺ ☺ ☺ ☺
Splash pad	
Slide	
Sandbox	

Each ☺ = 1 kid

DAY 24 Alphabetical order

Read the words in each group. Then write them in ABC order.

wish	too
pretty	sing
~~every~~	could
jump	many
give	great
funny	fly
hug	also

every
___

Boost your learning and save 20%!
Scan the QR code or visit
www.ixl.com/workbook/12s for details.

DAY 25

Number pattern maze

Help the fox find her den! Look at the number pattern so far. Color the path to continue the pattern.

START		1	3	5	7	9	11	4
		2	10	12	4	6	13	10
20	16	30	24	18	21	19	17	15	22
33	31	29	27	25	23	36	32	40	34
35	36	38	44	28	42	52	56	46	50
37	39	41	43	45	47	48	68	62	72
54	60	70	58	64	49	50	66	78	86
76	59	57	55	53	51	80	88	92	100
84	61	90	68	70	76	74	FINISH		
94	63	65	67	69	71	73			

ENRICHMENT

57

© IXL Learning

DAY 25 Crack the code

Can you crack the code? Use the picture clues to help.

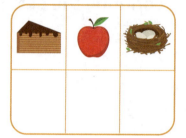
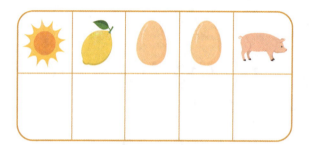
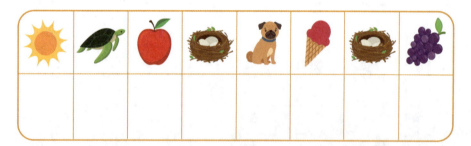

Picture clues

DAY 26 Add and subtract

IXL.com skill ID
Q8E

Follow the path from start to finish.

START

[7] →+4→ [ ] →−9→ [ ]
                              ↓ +8
[ ] ←−7← [ ]   [ ] →+6→ [ ]
↓ +8   ↑ +4   ↓ −8
[ ]   [ ] ←−6← [ ] ←+7← [ ]
↓ −10
[ ] →+6→ [ ] →+7→ [ ] →−8→ [9]
                                   FINISH

DAY 26 Silent -e words

Fill in the missing letters.

c		k	

k		t	

c		b	

b		n	

h		v	

r		b	

s		l		

f		l		

p		l		

DAY 27 Add three numbers

Add in two ways.

7 + 8 + 2
___15___ + 2 = ___17___

7 + 8 + 2
7 + ___10___ = ___17___

2 + 3 + 6
_____ + 6 = _____

2 + 3 + 6
2 + _____ = _____

8 + 5 + 3
_____ + 3 = _____

8 + 5 + 3
8 + _____ = _____

Add.

5 + 5 + 8 = _____

6 + 2 + 2 = _____

7 + 3 + 3 = _____

9 + 4 + 6 = _____

4 + 9 + 1 = _____

8 + 8 + 4 = _____

DAY 27 Real-life connections

IXL.com skill ID
9Q8

When you read a word, think about how it connects to other words or to your life. Making connections between words helps build your vocabulary.

Write three words you think of when you see each place.

zoo	fire station	park
lion		

Write two words that each adjective could describe.

round	fast	colorful
button wheel		
fluffy	mushy	brave

DAY 28 Picture graphs

IXL.com skill ID **QDT**

Violet asks her friends to pick their favorite zoo animals. She shows their answers on a picture graph.

Favorite zoo animal	
Bear	★ ★ ★
Tiger	★ ★ ★ ★
Lion	★ ★
Monkey	★ ★ ★ ★ ★

Each ★ = 1 friend

Answer each question.

How many friends picked monkeys? _____ friends

Which animal did the fewest friends pick? _____

How many friends in all picked tigers or bears? _____ friends

How many more friends picked monkeys than bears? _____ more friends

DAY 28: Ending punctuation

There are four types of sentences.

Sentence type	Punctuation
A **statement** tells about something.	.
A **question** asks about something.	?
An **exclamation** shows surprise or strong feelings.	!
A **command** tells someone to do something.	. or !

Write the correct ending punctuation. Then color the stars using the key.

BLUE statement   **GREEN** question   **PURPLE** exclamation   **YELLOW** command

Do you want to play a card game with me **?**

I always help clear the table after dinner ___

Wow, look at that amazing sunset ___

Please feed your pet rabbit ___

Where is Oklahoma on a map ___

Put your muddy shoes by the door ___

Fresh Mart is open every day ___

I can't wait for my birthday party ___

DAY 29 Weather and seasons

IXL.com skill ID
JEF

James lives in New York. Read about the weather in New York during each season. Then draw a picture of the season. Use details from the sentences to color your picture.

In the **winter**, it is cold and it might snow. Most trees do not have leaves on them.	In the **spring**, it gets warmer and it can be rainy. Grass turns green, plants grow, and flowers bloom.
In the **summer**, it is hot. Some flowers bloom, and many trees have green leaves.	In the **fall**, it gets cooler. Some leaves change to red or orange. Leaves also fall to the ground.

Look outside. What is the weather like today?

_____

_____

 **Brain Break!** Give yourself a big hug. Wrap your arms around yourself and hold for ten seconds.

DAY 29 Reading comprehension

Read the passage. Then answer the questions.

Frogs and Toads

Frogs and toads are both amphibians. This means they spend part of their lives in water and part on land. They eat bugs, slugs, and even small animals. Frogs and toads seem alike, but they have a few differences.

You can tell frogs and toads apart by looking at their skin. Frogs have smooth skin. Toads have bumpy, dry skin.

The two animals' legs are also different. A frog has long legs for jumping far and fast. A toad's legs are short for hopping or walking.

These amphibians are special in their own ways.

What type of animals are frogs and toads? _____

How are frogs and toads alike? Put an X next to the correct answer.

_____ They jump far.   _____ They eat bugs.   _____ They have dry skin.

How are frogs and toads different? Write your answers in the table.

Frogs	Toads
• jump far and fast • •	• hop and walk • •

DAY 30 Sudoku

Complete the sudoku puzzles using the numbers 1–4. Each number must appear only once in each row, column, and block.

4	1	3	2
2		1	
3	2	4	
1	4	2	3

2			1
	3	4	2
3			4
4	2		3

1	4	3	
		1	4
4	1		3
2		4	

		4	3
4			
2	1		4
3			2

ENRICHMENT

DAY 30 Square challenge

Let's get creative! Turn each square into an object, such as a present or a picture frame. How many objects can you draw in five minutes?

Weeks 7–9: Overview

Week 7

Math
Place value
Addition with tens and ones

Social studies
Cardinal directions

Language arts
Understanding characters
Antonyms
Prepositions

Enrichment
Decode the riddles
Logic puzzle

Week 8

Math
Compare and order numbers
Two-digit addition

Science
Living and nonliving things

Language arts
Short and long vowel sounds
Word relationships
Past, present, and future verbs

Enrichment
Picture puzzle
Find and count

Week 9

Math
Two-digit addition
Addition with missing digits

Social studies
Water features

Language arts
Reading informational text
Adjectives
Complete sentences

Enrichment
Alphabet search
Decoding words

More ways to learn

Keep the learning going! Use these simple, exciting activities to help you stay active, curious, and creative during your summer break.

See how many activities you can do! Cross off each activity as you complete it.

Create a picture collage about summer using old magazines. 	**Find a new book at your local library.** 	**Make a hat or crown out of paper.** 
Make a friendship bracelet for someone special. 	**Go outside to blow bubbles.** 	**Have a picnic in your backyard or at a nearby park.** 
Observe insects outside and draw what you see. 	**Write a different ending for your favorite movie.** 	**Play a board game with a family member.** 

DAY 31 — Vowel teams

IXL.com skill ID **BUQ**

Sometimes two vowels work together as a **vowel team**. The first vowel in a vowel team makes a long vowel sound. The second vowel is silent.

Complete each word with the correct vowel team. Some vowel teams will be used more than once.

| ai   ea   ee   ie   oa   ue |

t _ie_

s _ea_ l

g _oa_ l

m _ai_ l

b _oa_ t

b _lue_

d _ee_ r

b _ea_ n

t r _ai_ n

LANGUAGE ARTS

DAY 31 Cardinal directions

Maps have four directions. North is on the top. South is on the bottom. West is on the left. East is on the right.

Fill in the blanks with the missing direction: north, south, east, or west.

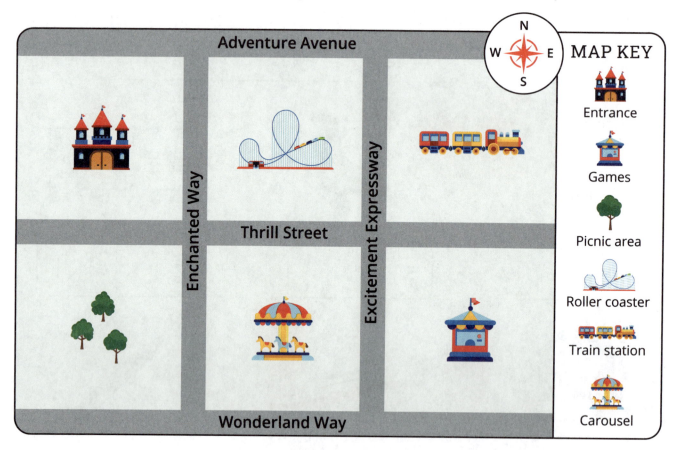

The entrance is _____ of the picnic area.

The carousel is _____ of the games.

Thrill Street is _____ of the roller coaster.

The train station is _____ of the roller coaster.

The picnic area is _____ of the carousel.

DAY 32 Reading comprehension

IXL.com skill ID
8G5

When you read, think about what the characters do and say. This can help you understand what the characters are like and how they feel.

Read the passages. Then put an X next to each correct answer.

On the way to summer camp, the kids on the bus shouted and laughed. Lina didn't say much, but she had a big smile.

What is Lina probably like?

_____ quiet _____ smart _____ bored

"It's time to dance!" Alex said. He took his sister's hand and bounced around the room.

What is Alex probably like?

_____ playful _____ brave _____ calm

Julia yawned and rolled over. She closed her eyes and said, "Just a few more minutes, Mom."

How does Julia probably feel?

_____ sad _____ sleepy _____ happy

Luke goes with his mom to pick up Uncle Paul from the airport. When he sees Uncle Paul, Luke waves and jumps up and down.

How does Luke probably feel?

_____ nervous _____ shy _____ excited

LANGUAGE ARTS © IXL Learning 73

DAY 32 Tens and ones

Fill in the blanks.

___4___ tens + ___3___ ones = ___43___

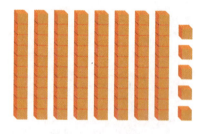

_____ tens + _____ ones = _____

_____ tens + _____ ones = _____

Fill in the blanks. Think about blocks to help.

___2___ tens + ___6___ ones = 26

_____ tens + _____ ones = 58

_____ tens + _____ ones = 37

_____ tens + _____ ones = 62

_____ tens + _____ ones = 90

_____ tens + _____ ones = 74

DAY 33

Antonyms

IXL.com skill ID
9TV

Antonyms are opposites. Color each diamond that has a pair of antonyms.

down / up

friendly / kind

near / far

after / before

close / shut

slow / fast

save / keep

never / always

behind / ahead

tell / ask

few / many

gentle / soft

 **Brain Break!** Think of a knock-knock joke. Now tell it to someone!

DAY 33 Tens and ones

Circle 10 ones blocks to make a ten. Then fill in the blanks to match the model.

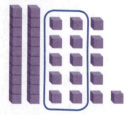

2 tens + 16 ones = __3__ tens + __6__ ones = __36__

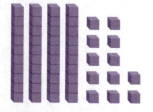

4 tens + 12 ones = _____ tens + _____ ones = _____

1 ten + 19 ones = _____ tens + _____ ones = _____

6 tens + 10 ones = _____ tens + _____ ones = _____

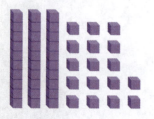

3 tens + 17 ones = _____ tens + _____ ones = _____

DAY 34 Prepositions

IXL.com skill ID
SXL

A **preposition** tells where something is or where something happens.

Complete each sentence with a preposition from the word bank. Each word will be used once.

| on | under | above | between | behind | ~~near~~ | beside |

The clock is _____ near _____ the window.

The window is _____ the desk.

The teddy bear is _____ the ball.

The desk is _____ the couch and the shelf.

The lamp is _____ the desk.

The rug is _____ the couch.

The dotted pillow is _____ the striped pillow.

LANGUAGE ARTS © IXL Learning

DAY 34 Tens and ones

Use 10 ones to make a ten. Then fill in the blanks to match the model.

~~3~~⁴ tens + ~~15~~⁵ ones = __4__ tens + __5__ ones = __45__

7 tens + 12 ones = _____ tens + _____ ones = _____

2 tens + 18 ones = _____ tens + _____ ones = _____

5 tens + 13 ones = _____ tens + _____ ones = _____

8 tens + 19 ones = _____ tens + _____ ones = _____

7 tens + 10 ones = _____ tens + _____ ones = _____

1 ten + 17 ones = _____ tens + _____ ones = _____

Explore hundreds more topics!
Get 20% off when you join IXL today.
Scan this QR code for details.

78

DAY 35
Decode the riddles

Solve the riddles. Write each letter of your answer on a line. You can use the secret code below to help you!

What can you catch but not throw?

A   C   O   L   D
10   4   13   8   15

What must be broken before you can use it?

___ ___ ___ ___ ___
10   6   11   7   7

What has a head and a tail but no bottom?

___ ___ ___ ___ ___
10   4   13   3   6

What gets wet as it dries?

___ ___ ___ ___ ___ ___
10   9   13   12   11   8

What fills a room without taking up space?

___ ___ ___ ___ ___
8   3   7   1   9

What goes up and down without moving?

___ ___ ___ ___ ___ ___
16   9   10   3   2   16

What goes up but never comes down?

___ ___ ___ ___ ___ ___ ___
14   13   5   2   10   7   11

1	2	3	4	5	6	7	8	9	10	11	12	13	14	15	16	17	18
H	R	I	C	U	N	G	L	T	A	E	W	O	Y	D	S	F	M

ENRICHMENT

DAY 35 Logic puzzle

Lisa, Xavier, Jade, and Eric are friends who all go to Cedar Cove Camp. Each friend has a different favorite camp activity.

Use the clues and grid to find out each friend's favorite camp activity.

- Eric does not like crafts or swimming.
- Lisa's favorite activity has all the letters in her name.
- Xavier likes making things with his hands.
- Jade's favorite activity is done in the camp's lake.

Friend	Camp activity			
	Soccer	Swimming	Crafts	Sailing
Lisa				
Xavier				
Jade				
Eric				

Use your answers from the grid to finish the sentences.

Lisa's favorite camp activity is _____.

Xavier's favorite camp activity is _____.

Jade's favorite camp activity is _____.

Eric's favorite camp activity is _____.

DAY 36 — Compare and order numbers

IXL.com skill ID
LK6

Fill in each circle with >, <, or = .

25 < 48   83 ◯ 68

87 ◯ 92   51 ◯ 51

24 ◯ 41   54 ◯ 48

21 ◯ 19   62 ◯ 71

74 ◯ 47   38 ◯ 37

Write each set of numbers in order from least to greatest.

43   26   58   _26_   _43_   _58_

93   74   87   ____   ____   ____

58   67   60   ____   ____   ____

30   28   34   24   ____   ____   ____   ____

64   60   46   16   ____   ____   ____   ____

88   83   96   92   ____   ____   ____   ____

81

DAY 36
Short and long vowel sounds

Read each word. Do you hear a short vowel sound or a long vowel sound? Color the clouds using the key.

BLUE — short vowel sound
YELLOW — long vowel sound

DAY 37: Living and nonliving things

Living things need water. They also need food or sunlight to make food. Living things grow and reproduce. **Nonliving things** do not need water or food. They do not grow or reproduce.

Each picture shows a living or nonliving thing. Circle the answer.

grass	hamster	rock
(living) nonliving	living nonliving	living nonliving
butterfly	**umbrella**	**sunflower**
living nonliving	living nonliving	living nonliving
flashlight	**train**	**goldfish**
living nonliving	living nonliving	living nonliving

 **Brain Break!** Can you walk like an animal? Try to walk like a frog. Now, try walking like a bear!

DAY 37 Reading comprehension

Read the story. Then answer the questions.

Mia's Great Garden

Mia the Mouse peeks out her window. It has rained every day for three weeks. She has not been able to get outside to plant a garden in her yard. When she sees the clear sky, she jumps up.

Knock! Knock! Ben the Bunny is at the door with his garden tools. "Do you see that? It's the sun! Can you believe it?" Ben asks with a big smile.

"I know! Now you can help me plant my garden!" Mia says. She gathers her seeds, tools, and gloves. Then Ben and Mia head to the backyard.

Mia and Ben spend hours making a garden in Mia's yard. They plant rows of flower seeds. Then they water the seeds. As they work, they laugh and talk. Before they know it, the sun starts to set. It is time for Ben to go home.

"Thank you for your help!" Mia says. She waves goodbye and goes inside to rest. It was a fun day making a great garden.

Why was Mia stuck inside? _____

_____

Why is Ben smiling when he arrives at Mia's door? Put an X next to the correct answer.

____ It is raining.   ____ The sun is shining.   ____ The garden is done.

What do Mia and Ben plant in the garden? _____

DAY 38 — Word relationships

IXL.com skill ID **R89**

Sort the words into groups.

~~sad~~   pants   joyful   shirt   upset   dress
cookies   grapes   nurse   teacher   popcorn   pilot

Feelings	Jobs
• sad	•
•	•
•	•

Things you wear	Snacks for a picnic
•	•
•	•
•	•

Read the words. Then write a name for each group.

_____	_____
• arm	• plane
• leg	• kite
• nose	• bird
• hand	• hot air balloon

LANGUAGE ARTS

DAY 38 Two-digit addition

Add.

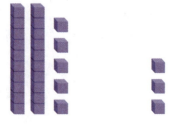

25 + 3 = _____

12 + 7 = _____

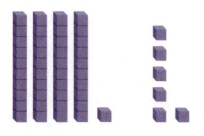

41 + 6 = _____

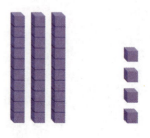

30 + 4 = _____

Add. Think about blocks to help.

57 + 2 = _____

23 + 3 = _____

60 + 8 = _____

14 + 5 = _____

36 + 1 = _____

42 + 4 = _____

73 + 5 = _____

91 + 7 = _____

DAY 39 — Past, present, and future

Read each sentence. Which verb tense does the sentence use? Color the stars using the key.

BLUE — past tense   **GREEN** — present tense   **PURPLE** — future tense

Next week, Ellie **will go** to her friend's party at the park. ☆

Felix **watched** the new TV show about bears in space. ☆

Meg **loves** the berries from Smith's Farm. ☆

Samir **painted** a picture as a gift for his friend. ☆

Logan and Beth **rode** their bikes to the park. ☆

Eve **waits** with her friends for the swim meet to begin. ☆

Rudra and Anika **will build** a fort in their yard. ☆

Write a sentence for each verb and verb tense.

jump past tense	
help present tense	
talk future tense	

DAY 39 Two-digit addition

Add. Start by making a ten with 10 ones.

27 + 6 = __33__

35 + 9 = _____

18 + 7 = _____

42 + 8 = _____

Add. Make a ten to help.

38 + 3 = _____   86 + 6 = _____

17 + 7 = _____   29 + 2 = _____

53 + 9 = _____   48 + 5 = _____

79 + 4 = _____   67 + 3 = _____

25 + 7 = _____   56 + 9 = _____

DAY 40

Math picture puzzle

Can you figure out the value of each picture? Each picture has the same value across the equations.

$$2 \quad + \quad \text{(sun)} \quad = \quad 18$$

$$\text{(sun)} \quad - \quad \text{(umbrella)} \quad = \quad 9$$

$$\text{(popsicle)} \quad - \quad 13 \quad = \quad \text{(umbrella)}$$

$$\text{(turtle)} \quad + \quad \text{(turtle)} \quad = \quad \text{(popsicle)}$$

$$\text{(sunglasses)} \quad + \quad \text{(turtle)} \quad = \quad \text{(sun)}$$

$$\text{(starfish)} \quad - \quad \text{(umbrella)} \quad = \quad \text{(sunglasses)}$$

Write the value of each picture.

(sun) = _____   (umbrella) = _____   (popsicle) = _____

(turtle) = _____   (sunglasses) = _____   (starfish) = _____

ENRICHMENT

DAY 40 Find and count

Count the number of times you see each image. Then write the total below.

DAY 41 Reading comprehension

Read the passage. Then answer the questions.

Penguins at the Beach

Have you ever seen penguins on a beach? You might think of penguins living in the ice and snow. But penguins can also live in warm places!

Some penguins live on a beach in Africa called Boulders Beach. It is named Boulders Beach because of its large rocks, or **boulders**. The rocks are in the sand and the water.

The boulders help keep the penguins safe. The penguins hide behind the rocks, away from the wind and other animals. The boulders keep the penguins' nests and babies out of sight, too.

The calm water at Boulders Beach is also good for penguins. The penguins swim, play, and hunt for food in the gentle waves.

In the text, underline the sentence that tells what penguins do in the water.

What does the word **boulders** mean? Put an X next to the correct answer.

___ penguin eggs ___ large rocks ___ sandy beaches

Why is Boulders Beach a good home for penguins? Write **two** reasons.

1.
2.

LANGUAGE ARTS © IXL Learning 91

DAY 41 — Two-digit addition

IXL.com skill ID **TX5**

Add. Start by adding the ones digits. Then add the tens digits.

```
  3 6        4 0        6 2
+ 2 1      +   9      +   6
-----      -----      -----
  5 7
```

```
  2 0        5 1        2 3
+   3      +   8      +   4
-----      -----      -----
```

```
  1 7        1 2        7 0
+ 2 1      + 2 5      + 1 3
-----      -----      -----
```

Write the missing digits.

```
  2 8        ☐ 4        1 9
+ 3 ☐      + 4 4      + ☐ 0
-----      -----      -----
  5 9        9 8        7 9
```

```
  4 ☐        3 3        8 ☐
+ 2 2      + ☐ 1      + ☐ 4
-----      -----      -----
  ☐ 7        7 ☐        9 6
```

DAY 42

Long vowel words

IXL.com skill ID
LLR

Follow the long vowel words to help the dog find his doghouse. No diagonal moves are allowed.

START

	brave	fell	flip	ant
nick	heal	blob	crust	bus
home	mice	moss	went	help
tube	cling	just	doll	lock
wait	pay	scene	queen	tried
lunch	bump	hand	dust	coal
truck	milk	smell	true	eve
loss	space	low	sweet	print
hill	twice	fix	chest	dash
dusk	green	age	blue	

FINISH

LANGUAGE ARTS © IXL Learning 93

DAY 42 Two-digit addition

Add. Start by adding the ones digits and making a ten. Then add the tens digits.

```
  1
  3 5          6 5           2 6
+ 2 7        +   6         +   8
-----        -----         -----
  6 2
```

```
  4 5          2 8           5 2
+   5        +   7         +   9
-----        -----         -----
```

```
  1 7          2 3           3 4
+ 2 6        + 2 8         + 5 6
-----        -----         -----
```

Write the missing digits.

```
   1
   3  8         6  4          ☐  9
+ [2] 5       + ☐  7        + 4  1
--------      --------      --------
   6  3          8  1          7  0
```

```
   ☐  6          5  4          ☐  7
+  6  9       +  ☐  8       +  4  7
--------      --------      --------
   9  ☐          7  ☐          8  ☐
```

94

DAY 43 Adjectives

An **adjective** tells about a person, animal, place, or thing. Adjectives tell you **what kind** or **how many**.

Circle the adjective in each sentence.

Amir sees a (big) crab.

I counted eleven shells.

My clean clothes are in the bag.

The kite has a long string.

The tall waves crash on the beach.

Jess ran on the yellow sand.

Owen gets two shovels for the bucket.

Write two adjectives that describe each picture.

ice cream

_____

_____

spoon

_____

_____

cherries

_____

_____

DAY 43 Water features

Read about the water features below. Then label each water feature.

Water feature	About
ocean	a large body of salt water
bay	a body of water partly surrounded by land
lake	a body of water with land all around
waterfall	water falling from a high place
river	water that moves in a line across the land
stream	a small river

stream   _____   _____

_____   _____   _____

DAY 44 — Sentence scramble

Write the words in the correct order to make a sentence. Remember to use correct capitalization and end punctuation.

feels sleepy Tom

Tom feels sleepy.

loves She pizza

tree a plants Alvin

made Emily snack a

cows baby Calves are

the park ran around We

ten cakes The baker made

day fell The rain long all

 Wink with your left eye and snap with your right hand. Now switch! How fast can you go?

DAY 44 Tic-tac-toe addition

Find the row, column, or diagonal line where all of the sums are the same.

53 + 6 = 59	17 + 24 = 41	45 + 31 = 76
23 + 57 = 80	67 + 9 = 76	82 + 6 = 88
18 + 58 = 76	51 + 45 = 96	64 + 19 = 83

(diagonal line drawn through 45+31, 67+9, 18+58)

81 + 3	13 + 35	36 + 24
45 + 27	39 + 9	34 + 12
23 + 26	26 + 22	63 + 8

12 + 35	37 + 26	65 + 9
74 + 6	53 + 4	11 + 46
58 + 35	88 + 5	49 + 44

38 + 27	13 + 42	54 + 6
67 + 13	56 + 9	45 + 21
70 + 16	37 + 44	61 + 4

DAY 45

Alphabet search

It's time for an alphabet search! Find or think of an item that begins with each letter. Write the name of each item next to the letter.

A		N	
B		O	
C		P	
D		Q	
E		R	
F		S	
G		T	
H		U	
I		V	
J		W	
K		X	
L		Y	
M		Z	

ENRICHMENT

DAY 45 · Mystery words

Can you decode the mystery words? Use the first letter of the object shown in the image to discover each word.

C	I	T	Y

100 · © IXL Learning · ENRICHMENT

Weeks 10–12: Overview

Week 10

Math
Telling time
Two-digit subtraction

Science
Plant parts

Language arts
Related words
R-controlled vowels
Past-tense verbs

Enrichment
Fill-in-the-blank story
Math puzzles

Week 11

Math
Subtracting tens
Subtraction word problems

Social studies
Goods and services

Language arts
Text features
Context clues
Articles

Enrichment
Color the time
Rhyming words

Week 12

Math
Measurement
Addition and subtraction word problems

Science
Animal groups

Language arts
Reading poetry
Compound words
Pronoun-verb agreement

Enrichment
Logic puzzle
Summer reflections

More ways to learn

Keep the learning going! Use these simple, exciting activities to help you stay active, curious, and creative during your summer break.

See how many activities you can do! Cross off each activity as you complete it.

Create a puppet with a paper bag. 	**Invent a new sport and try it out.** 	**Go camping in your living room.** 
Build a tower using playing cards. 	**Make a card for a friend.** 	**Play volleyball with a balloon.** 
Write a story about your favorite summer adventure so far. 	**Try a new food with a family member and write a review.** 	**Decorate a bookmark with your name and favorite colors.** 

Day 46: Word problems

Answer each question.

Naomi goes to the dog park. She sees 11 dogs playing and 8 dogs resting. How many total dogs does Naomi see at the dog park?

_____ dogs

Mr. Garcia digs holes to plant bushes and trees in his yard. He digs 14 holes for bushes and 7 holes for trees. How many holes does Mr. Garcia dig in all?

_____ holes

Ms. Abara is frosting cupcakes. She frosts 24 of them with pink frosting and 36 of them with blue frosting. How many total cupcakes does Ms. Abara frost?

_____ cupcakes

Nina and Clara are at a pool. Nina jumps in the pool 26 times. Clara jumps in the pool 25 times. How many times do Nina and Clara jump in the pool in all?

_____ times

Louis bikes to a lake. He takes 19 pictures on the way to the lake. He takes 48 pictures at the lake. How many pictures does Louis take altogether?

_____ pictures

DAY 46 Related words

Some words are alike but have small differences in meaning. **Run** and **walk** are alike. They are both ways you can move, but running is faster than walking.

Read each question and circle the correct answer.

Which is shorter?	a minute	an hour
Which is older?	a dog	a puppy
Which is taller?	a hill	a mountain
Which happens first?	the middle	the start
Which is louder?	shouting	talking

Put the words in order. Write them in the boxes below.

year, ~~day~~, week

day		

shortest — longest

pond, ocean, lake

smallest — biggest

child, grandma, parent

youngest — oldest

DAY 47 — Telling time

Write the time shown on each clock.

4:00   _____   _____

_____   _____   _____

Draw hands on each clock to show the time.

 Count from one to twenty. Then count backward from twenty to one!

Reading comprehension

Read the story. Then answer the questions.

A Song Worth Sharing

Jamie was a joyful, friendly bird who lived in the forest. His friends loved to sing together. Jamie wanted to sing with them. But he was shy about his voice.

One day, a bird named Lola came to the forest. Jamie was excited to make a new friend! He said hello and told Lola all about the forest. Her eyes lit up when he told her about the singing.

"I love to sing!" said Lola. "But I don't know anyone here. I'm afraid to sing with the other birds." Lola looked sad.

"I'm also shy about singing with everyone," said Jamie. "Maybe we can sing together! Then it won't seem so scary," he said.

Lola thought that was a great idea! They flew to where the others were already singing. Jamie and Lola joined in quietly at first. Then Lola sang louder, so Jamie did too.

Lola smiled at Jamie. They had helped each other to be brave.

Why doesn't Jamie sing with the other birds?

_____

What is the lesson of this story? Put an X next to the correct answer.

_____ Hard work always pays off.

_____ Singing by yourself is better than singing together.

_____ It is easier to face something new with someone else.

DAY 48 Two-digit subtraction

Cross out blocks to model the subtraction. Then write the difference.

 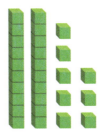

54 − 3 = __51__   28 − 5 = _____

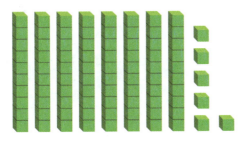   

86 − 2 = _____   39 − 6 = _____

Subtract. Think about blocks to help.

19 − 8 = _____   85 − 3 = _____

58 − 5 = _____   79 − 6 = _____

66 − 4 = _____   24 − 4 = _____

47 − 5 = _____   96 − 5 = _____

DAY 48: R-controlled vowels

IXL.com skill ID
WSL

An **r-controlled vowel** is a vowel that is followed by the letter **r**. The **r** changes the sound of the vowel. Some r-controlled vowels are **ar**, **er**, **ir**, **or**, and **ur**.

Use the key to color the picture.

- **PINK** — ar words
- **PURPLE** — er words
- **YELLOW** — ir words
- **ORANGE** — or words
- **GREEN** — ur words

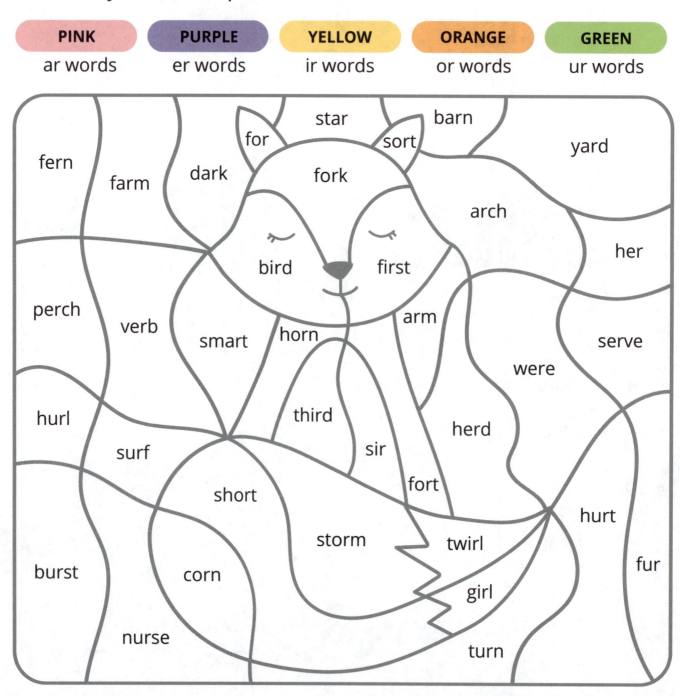

108 © IXL Learning   LANGUAGE ARTS

DAY 49 Plant parts

IXL.com skill ID
KDK

Plants are made up of different parts. These parts help the plant make food, get water, grow, and make new plants.

Complete the crossword puzzle. Use the word bank to help you.

Word bank
- ~~fruit~~
- seeds
- leaves
- roots
- flowers
- stem

Across:

1. This holds the seeds. F R U I T

4. These turn into fruit. ___ ___ ___ ___ ___ ___ ___

6. These are where the plant makes most of its food.
   ___ ___ ___ ___ ___ ___

Down:

2. These hold the plant in the soil. ___ ___ ___ ___ ___

3. These grow into new plants. ___ ___ ___ ___ ___

5. This holds the plant up above the ground. ___ ___ ___ ___

SCIENCE

Day 49: Past-tense verbs

Fill in the blanks. Write the past-tense form of each verb.

We _____watched_____ Addie's brother do a bunch of magic tricks.
       watch

I _____ the gate behind me when I left the backyard.
   close

Aunt Sue _____ us with plans to go bowling.
     surprise

We _____ around the huge garden for hours.
   walk

The birds _____ easily on the wet rocks.
    land

Cora _____ her room blue with yellow stripes.
    paint

Joe _____ the exact number of marbles in the jar!
   guess

I _____ the salty beach air as soon as I got out of the car.
  smell

Wyatt _____ his backpack for his first plane ride.
   pack

Liza and Mitch _____ the new ice cream flavor.
    taste

Become an IXL member for unlimited practice. Join today!
Scan the QR code or visit www.ixl.com/workbook/12s for details.

DAY 50

Fill-in-the-blank story

Complete the story! First, fill in the blanks using the key. Use each word only once. Then read your silly story out loud!

🏓	🦈	🕶️	👒
boots	cheetah	danced	fuzzy
cookies	giraffe	hopped	muddy
kites	rabbit	tumbled	hungry
oranges	snail	zoomed	sparkly
rocks	turtle	giggled	stinky

In a _____ animal town, Speedy the _____ and 👒

Hoppy the _____ decided to race. Everyone _____, 🦈 🕶️

knowing Hoppy was super _____. "Ready, set, go!" 👒

Hoppy _____ ahead, but Speedy had a secret. He wore 🕶️

_____ roller skates! As Hoppy stopped for _____, 👒 🏓

Speedy _____ past. The crowd cheered loudly as Speedy 🕶️

_____ across the finish line first. Hoppy _____ up 🕶️ 🕶️

to Speedy and exclaimed, "Best race ever!" And from then on, they raced every

weekend, sharing _____ and _____. 🏓 🏓

ENRICHMENT

111

© IXL Learning

DAY 50 — Math puzzles

Each puzzle uses the numbers 1–9 once. If you add across, you get the number on the right. If you add down, you get the number on the bottom. Fill in the missing numbers.

5	8	1	14
	2	4	12
3	7		19
14	17	14	

	2		16
3		4	8
	7	8	21
18	10	17	

	4	5	16
1			12
	8	3	17
14	21	10	

8			16
4		3	14
	9	5	15
13	18	14	

1			12
	7	4	17
2		5	16
9	24	12	

9		4	19
	1		11
5			15
17	15	13	

112

© IXL Learning

ENRICHMENT

DAY 51 Reading comprehension

IXL.com skill ID
YCR

Some books have a **glossary**. The glossary is near the back of the book. It lists important words used in the book, and it tells you what they mean.

Read the glossary from a book about meerkats. Then answer the questions. Put an X next to each correct answer.

Glossary

burrow	a hole or tunnel where meerkats live and hide
colony	a group of meerkats that live together
foraging	looking for food
pup	a baby meerkat
sentry	a meerkat that watches out for danger

How are the words in the glossary organized?

_____ ABC order

_____ cause and effect

_____ most important to least important

Which informational text is the glossary most like?

_____ an article   _____ a dictionary   _____ a map

What does **sentry** mean?

_____ a baby meerkat

_____ a group of meerkats that live together

_____ a meerkat that watches out for danger

Where do meerkats live? _____

LANGUAGE ARTS

113

© IXL Learning

DAY 51 Subtracting tens

Cross out blocks to model the subtraction. Then write the difference.

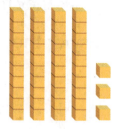

43 − 20 = _____

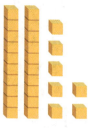

27 − 10 = _____

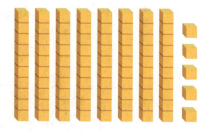

85 − 50 = _____

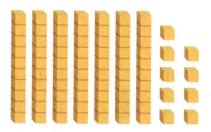

79 − 70 = _____

Subtract. Think about blocks to help.

92 − 60 = _____   66 − 50 = _____

44 − 20 = _____   18 − 10 = _____

51 − 40 = _____   70 − 50 = _____

25 − 20 = _____   67 − 40 = _____

DAY 52 Syllables

IXL.com skill ID
M6D

You can break a word into syllables. Each **syllable** has one vowel sound. For example, **window** has two vowel sounds, so it has two syllables.

Say the words aloud. Write the number of syllables you hear in each word.

candle	bear	cookie	volcano	butterfly	key
2	___	___	___	___	___

Read the words in the maze. Follow the two-syllable words from start to finish. No diagonal moves are allowed.

START

after	funny	going	help	long
please	small	began	bumpy	click
bring	cry	land	garden	night
without	summer	penny	number	place
broken	chase	edge	kept	proud

FINISH

Brain Break! Hop on one foot ten times. Hop on your other foot ten times. Now, hop on both feet ten times!

DAY 52: Goods and services

Everything you buy is a good or service. A **good** is a thing you can hold or touch. A **service** is a job someone can do for you.

Each picture shows a good or a service. Circle the answer.

DAY 53 Context clues

Context clues are nearby words that help you figure out the meaning of a new word.

Use context clues to help you figure out the meaning of each bold word. Circle the answer.

We **harvested** the ripe cherries, placing them carefully in buckets.	(picked)	ate	planted
Mae can't wait for practice! She is **eager** to meet her new team.	excited	lost	fresh
The desert looks **vast** outside the airplane window. It goes on and on.	brown	large	outside
Conrad rubbed his eyes. He was **weary** after the long car ride.	excited	upset	tired
If you have some wood and nails, you can **construct** a garden bed.	build	water	find

Write the meaning of the bold word on the line.

Stella is a **swift** swimmer. She wins many races. _____

Zac is a wonderful artist. I **adore** his colorful paintings. _____

Sunflowers are **lofty**. Their stems often stretch high above the ground. _____

117

DAY 53
Two-digit subtraction

Subtract.

```
  17          39          83
-  3        -  6        - 20
```

```
  61          24          55
-  1        - 10        -  4
```

```
  76          98          40
- 50        -  7        - 20
```

Write the missing numbers.

```
  7 ☐          3 7          6 4
-   5        - ☐          - ☐ 0
-----        -----        -----
  7 4          3 1          3 4
```

```
  ☐ 3          9 ☐          ☐ 5
- 2 ☐        - ☐ 0        - ☐
-----        -----        -----
    3          2 5          4 3
```

DAY 54 Articles

The words **a**, **an**, and **the** are called **articles**. These words come before nouns.

Circle the articles in each sentence.

We watched (the) huge whales from (a) boat.

When I bring a cake into the room, we will yell, "Surprise!"

Jill likes to dip an apple in peanut butter for a snack.

She made an octopus and a seahorse out of balloons.

Next summer, we'll use the rope swing to jump in the water.

The articles **a** and **an** are used before singular nouns that are not specific.

- Use **a** if the next word starts with a consonant sound, like **dog**.
- Use **an** if the next word starts with a vowel sound, like **apple**.

Complete each sentence with a or an.

I have always wanted to ride __a__ zip line through the woods!

Mila saw _____ airplane take off and disappear into the clouds.

The dog made such _____ mess when he tipped over the trash can.

I need to make _____ card for Mom, but I don't know what to draw.

Tim said _____ animal just ran into the yard and jumped in the pool!

DAY 54 Word problems

Answer each question.

Lena gets 15 toys for her dog, Bo. Then Bo loses 3 toys. How many toys does Bo have now?

_____ toys

Ren has a bin with 38 colored pencils. He gives 5 colored pencils to his sister. How many colored pencils are in the bin now?

_____ colored pencils

Mary picks 56 strawberries. She eats 20 of them. How many strawberries are left?

_____ strawberries

Amari has a sheet of 75 stickers. He uses 20 of them on a picture. How many stickers does the sheet have now?

_____ stickers

Ms. Cruz has 29 balloons. She gives 5 balloons to Chris. How many balloons does Ms. Cruz have now?

_____ balloons

Exclusive offer!
Explore hundreds more topics! Get 20% off when you join IXL today. Scan this QR code for details.

DAY 55 Color the time

Use the key to color the picture.

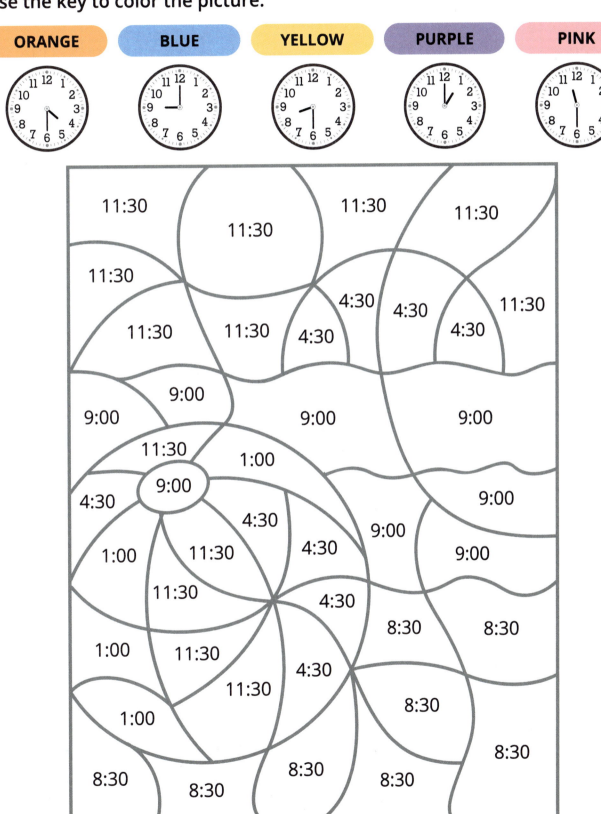

ENRICHMENT

DAY 55
Rhyming words tic-tac-toe

Find the row, column, or diagonal line where all three words rhyme.

band	ape	ham
rack	grand	bash
aid	clay	hand

sing	hill	dig
sink	king	pig
this	bring	big

bear	care	please
eat	heard	there
dear	near	year

show	down	cow
how	brown	grow
know	town	now

blue	huge	fruit
glue	suit	juice
true	tune	tube

glad	game	gray
buy	stay	fly
play	plane	pad

round	hour	four
our	sound	out
cloud	count	found

friend	met	went
pen	when	men
each	flew	deck

122 © IXL Learning

ENRICHMENT

Measuring inches

DAY 56

Use a ruler to measure each item to the nearest inch.

The whistle is _____ inches long.

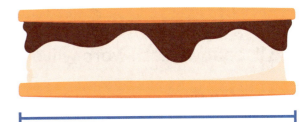

The s'more is _____ inches long.

The craft stick is _____ inches long.

The bracelet is _____ inches long.

Answer the questions.

How much longer is the bracelet than the whistle?   _____ inches longer

Jason puts the end of the craft stick next to the end of the s'more so that they touch. How long are the two items together?   _____ inches

DAY 56 Question words

Questions often start with a question word such as **who**, **what**, **when**, **where**, or **why**.

Complete each sentence with the best question word from the list above. Each word will be used once.

_____*What*_____ is your favorite food?

_____ did you get up this morning?

_____ is your favorite place to eat?

_____ is your best friend?

_____ should people brush their teeth?

Create your own questions using the words below. Remember to use a question mark at the end of each question.

What *did you do yesterday?*_____

When _____

Why _____

Where _____

DAY 57 Addition and subtraction

IXL.com skill ID
JDT

Find the row, column, or diagonal line where all of the sums and differences are the same.

61 −10	14 +27	32 +29		87 −30	68 + 7	36 +22
56 − 6	49 − 8	21 +40		47 − 4	14 +43	95 −50
19 +43	11 +30	64 −30		16 + 5	17 −10	59 − 2

49 −30	19 +51	62 + 6		39 − 9	83 −50	59 + 1
86 −40	35 +27	76 − 6		64 +11	27 +33	45 − 2
33 +30	58 + 5	67 − 4		80 −20	48 +33	51 + 4

DAY 57 Reading poetry

Read the poem. Then answer the questions.

Who Plays at Night?

Who's snoring in their nests?
Who's nicely tucked away?
The sun is down. And while it rests,
The owls come out to play.

The bats stretch out their wings.
And foxes start to prowl.
The crickets begin to sing their songs
As wolves begin to howl.

What is the poem about? Put an X next to the correct answer.

____ sunrise   ____ caves   ____ nighttime

Write **three** animals that are awake in the poem.

_____

Write **two** animals making noises in the poem.

_____

Look at the last word on each line of the poem. Some of the words rhyme, like **nests** and **rests**. Write another pair of rhyming words from the poem.

_____

DAY 58 Word problems

Ana is having a pool party! Answer each question.

Ana and her dad fill water balloons. Ana fills 28 balloons. Her dad fills 47 balloons. How many balloons do they fill in all?

_____ balloons

There are 18 kids in the pool. Then 10 kids get out of the pool. How many kids stay in the pool?

_____ kids

In a swimming race, the first team finishes in 30 seconds. The second team finishes in 49 seconds. How much longer does it take the second team to finish than the first team?

_____ seconds longer

Ana's dad grills 15 hot dogs. Then he grills 16 more hot dogs. How many hot dogs does Ana's dad grill altogether?

_____ hot dogs

Ana opens a box of 28 ice pops to share. After the party, there are 8 ice pops left. How many ice pops were eaten during the party?

_____ ice pops

 **Brain Break!** See what you can find around you! Can you find something red, something wooden, and something soft?

DAY 58 Compound words

A **compound word** is made from two smaller words.

Use the pictures to write the compound words.

 = cupcake

 + = _____

 + = _____

 + = _____

 + = _____

 + = _____

Draw a line to separate the two words that make each compound word.

flash|light   football   ladybug   popcorn   doghouse

DAY 59 Animal groups

Animals can be grouped based on traits they have in common.
Birds, **mammals**, **fish**, **reptiles**, and **amphibians** are groups of animals.

Animal group	Traits
Birds	Birds have feathers, two wings, and a beak.
Mammals	Mammals have hair or fur. They feed their young milk.
Fish	Fish live underwater. They have fins.
Reptiles	Reptiles have scaly, waterproof skin. Most live on land.
Amphibians	Amphibians have moist skin. They begin their lives in water.

Look at each picture. Then write the animal group.

bullfrog

amphibian

sand gecko

blue jay

red panda

guppy

red salamander

SCIENCE

DAY 59 Pronoun-verb agreement

Circle the correct verb or pronoun to complete each sentence.

They (sell) | sells umbrellas at the front of the store.

We | He smile for our family picture.

She make | makes new friends every summer at Wild Woods Camp.

She | You ride horses at Lone Oak Ranch, right?

I want | wants to learn how to bake an apple pie.

We | He likes the new movie about bears going to the moon.

We always sing | sings silly songs on long car rides.

I | He enjoy going to soccer games with my aunt.

It actually look | looks like the rain might stop soon.

She | They grow plants on the porch in the summer.

Complete each sentence with the correct pronoun.

__He__ watches shooting stars through his telescope.

_____ shares a piece of pie with her friend.

_____ visit the museum with our babysitter each week.

_____ give flowers to my grandma.

DAY 60 Logic puzzle

Lucy and some friends are eating together. They each have a lunchbox with a snack inside.

Use the clues and grid to find out which food item is in each lunchbox.

- The hummus is in a lunchbox with a color ending in **w**.
- One snack has the same name as its lunchbox color.
- One other snack starts with the same letter as its lunchbox color.

Snack	Lunchbox color			
	Yellow	Green	Pink	Orange
Hummus				
Pretzels				
Orange				
Crackers				

Use your answers from the grid to finish the sentences.

The hummus is in the _____ lunchbox.

The pretzels are in the _____ lunchbox.

The orange is in the _____ lunchbox.

The crackers are in the _____ lunchbox.

ENRICHMENT

DAY 60

My summer

Write about your summer!

This summer, I visited

I learned how to

I spent time with

The weather this summer was

If I could make one wish for next summer, it would be

The best thing I ate this summer was

Draw two memories from this summer.

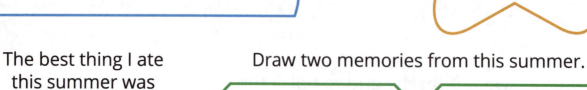

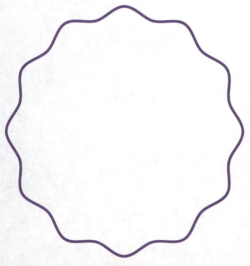

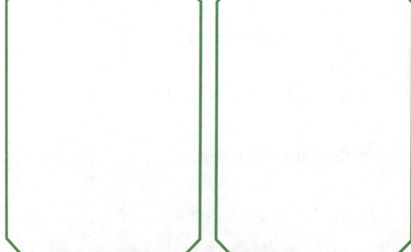

ENRICHMENT

Answer key

PAGE 7

Answers will vary.

PAGE 8

6	5
10	9
3	6
5	1
0	9
8	1
9	10
2	6
4	7
1	3

PAGE 9

bed	**j**am	**g**u**m**
lamp	**sh**e**d**	**cr**ab
map	**t**en**t**	**m**il**k**
wi**ng**	**t**an**k**	**h**an**d**

PAGE 10

Park Road

Bike rental

5

PAGE 11

PAGE 12

7 + 4 = 11

6 + 7 = 13

3 + 9 = 12

14	13
12	17

PAGE 13

tents

cones

lakes

flowers

bees

foxes

PAGE 13 *(continued)*

sisters

kites

brushes

peaches

PAGE 14

6, 7, **8**, 9, 10, **11**

17, **18**, 19, 20, **21**, 22

48, **49**, 50, **51**, 52, **53**

64, 65, **66**, **67**, 68, **69**

79, **80**, 81, **82**, **83**, 84

96, **97**, **98**, 99, **100**, **101**

106, **107**, 108, **109**, **110**, 111

115, 116, **117**, 118, **119**, **120**

PAGE 15

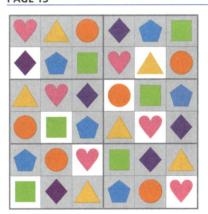

PAGE 16

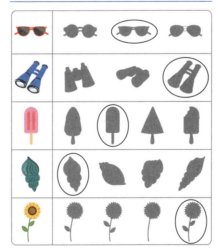

PAGE 17

sea	plane	red	bee
deer	rose	flew	sun
cent	stairs	road	flower

Answers will vary.

PAGE 18

3 + 5   7 + 3
4 + 6   8 + 8
9 + 5   2 + 6
5 + 7   10 + 4
7 + 8   4 + 8
6 + 10   9 + 9
7 + 6   9 + 6
10 + 8   8 + 5

PAGE 19

1

3

2

3

1

2

2

3

1

4

3

1

4

2

PAGE 20

| Vertices: 4 | Vertices: 3 |
| Sides: 4 | Sides: 3 |

| Vertices: 5 | Vertices: 4 |
| Sides: 5 | Sides: 4 |

| Vertices: 4 | Vertices: 6 |
| Sides: 4 | Sides: 6 |

triangle

square or rhombus

Answer key

PAGE 21
verb
noun
verb
noun
noun
verb
noun
verb

Answers will vary.

PAGE 22
pull	push	pull
pull	push	push
push	pull	push

PAGE 23

9	+	2	=	11		7	
+						+	
7	+	8	=	15		7	
=		+				=	
16		8	+	6	=	14	
		=		+			
		16		4			
				=			
				10	+	8	=	18
						+	
4		3		7	+	5	=	12
+		+				=	
4		6	+	7	=	13	
=		=					
8	+	9	=	17			

PAGE 24
fan	web	hill
pot	pig	frog
bat	bus	duck
vest	belt	mask

PAGE 25

1	2	3	4	5	6	7	8	9	10
11	12	13	14	15	16	17	18	19	20
21	22	23	24	25	26	27	28	29	30
31	32	33	34	35	36	37	38	39	40
41	42	43	44	45	46	47	48	49	50
51	52	53	54	55	56	57	58	59	60
61	62	63	64	65	66	67	68	69	70
71	72	73	74	75	76	77	78	79	80
81	82	83	84	85	86	87	88	89	90
91	92	93	94	95	96	97	98	99	100

PAGE 26
Elephants spend a lot of time near water. They love taking mud baths!

PAGE 27
club	flag	pond
raft	bolt	swing
brick	dress	block
trunk	plant	stamp

PAGE 28
6 + 6 = 12 cookies
5 + 8 = 13 kids
7 + 4 = 11 shells
9 + 7 = 16 apples
3 + 9 = 12 flowers

PAGE 29
Ari

Drawings will vary.

PAGE 30
12 − 4 = 8
16 − 7 = 9
18 − 8 = 10

| 7 | 3 |
| 6 | 7 |

PAGE 31
O	F
F	O
F	O
O	F

Answers will vary.

PAGE 32

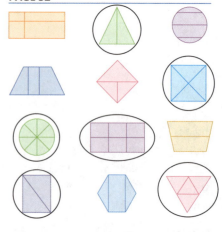

PAGE 33
(He) played in the pool with (them) for hours yesterday.

(I) gave (her) a birthday present.

(She) is taking (us) to the zoo this weekend.

Dad, can (you) read this book to (me) tonight?

(We) saw a show in the park, and (it) was a lot of fun!

(He) asked if (they) wanted to join (him) for a bike ride.

(I) think (we) should get (them) some popcorn, too.

Answers will vary.

PAGE 34
| valley | plain | island |
| mountain | canyon | hill |

PAGE 35
Drawings will vary.

134 © IXL Learning

Answer key

PAGE 36

		Pool float		
		Dinosaur	Flamingo	Donut
Friend	Sasha	X	●	X
	Levi	●	X	X
	Jordan	X	X	●

flamingo
dinosaur
donut

PAGE 39

3 + 5 = **8**   10 − 6 = **4**
8 − 3 = 5   6 + **4** = 10
12 − 2 = **10**   8 + 8 = **16**
2 + **10** = 12   **16** − 8 = 8
7 + 4 = **11**   13 − **8** = 5
11 − 7 = 4   **8** + 5 = 13
5 + 10 = 15   **13** − 6 = 7
15 − **5** = 10   6 + 7 = **13**
11 − **6** = 5   **9** + 8 = 17
6 + 5 = 11   17 − **9** = 8

PAGE 40

do**ll**   ro**ck**   be**ll**
bu**zz**   gra**ss**   cli**ff**
tr**uck**   fl**oss**   cr**ack**

Answers will vary.

PAGE 41

liquid   solid   solid
liquid   liquid   solid
liquid   solid   liquid

PAGE 42

PAGE 43

7 − 2
12 − 6
14 − 10
16 − 8
12 − 9
18 − 9
15 − 5
14 − 7

9 − 5
10 − 7
15 − 9
13 − 4
14 − 6
12 − 5
13 − 8
19 − 9

PAGE 44

cat   hose   pear
sink   nest   vase
lemon   earth   bread
stone   plate   steak

PAGE 45

Answers will vary. Some possible answers are shown below.

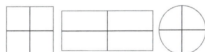

PAGE 46

We packed our things and moved to a new house.

Bruno carefully used the scissors.

Laura took a picture of her dog playing.

PAGE 47

honey   paper
mud   map
nest   sound

PAGE 48

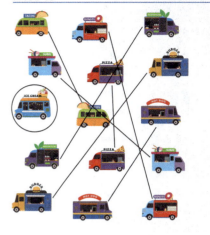

PAGE 49

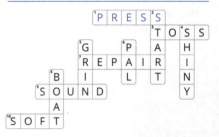

Across
1. PRESS
3. TOSS
7. REPAIR
9. SOUND
10. SOFT

Down
2. START
4. SHINY
5. GRIN
6. PAL
8. BOAT

PAGE 50

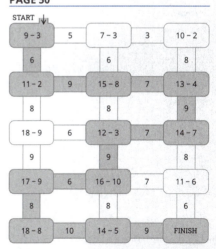

PAGE 51

chest   **f**i**sh**   **m**o**th**
phone   **sh**elf   **wh**ale
brush   pea**ch**   **ph**oto
whisk   cloth   ben**ch**

135

© IXL Learning

Answer key

PAGE 52

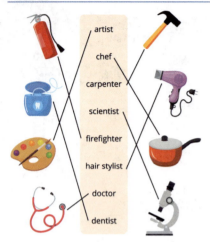

PAGE 53

10 − 5 = 5 ducks
11 − 9 = 2 more chickens
12 − 4 = 8 eggs
16 − 6 = 10 more crayons
13 − 7 = 6 kids

PAGE 54

collecting stickers and coins
Sample answer: to gather one kind of thing
places, people
Answers will vary.

PAGE 55

Where kids are playing at the park	
Swings	☺☺☺
Splash pad	☺☺☺☺☺☺
Slide	☺☺
Sandbox	☺☺☺☺☺

PAGE 56

every — also
funny — could
give — fly
hug — great
jump — many
pretty — sing
wish — too

PAGE 57

START	1	3	5	7	9	11	4
	2	10	12	4	6	13	10
20	16	30	24	18	21	19	17	15	22
33	31	29	27	25	23	36	32	40	34
35	36	38	44	28	42	52	56	46	50
37	39	41	43	45	47	48	68	62	72
54	60	70	58	64	49	50	66	78	86
76	59	57	55	53	51	80	88	92	100
84	61	90	68	70	76	74			FINISH
94	63	65	67	69	71	73			

PAGE 58

Horses can
sleep
standing up!

PAGE 59

START
7 +4→ 11 −9→ 2
↓ +8
6 ←−7 13 10 +6→ 16
↓ +8 ↑ +4   ↓ −8
14 9 ←−6 15 +7→ 8
↓ −10
4 +6→ 10 +7→ 17 −8→ 9
FINISH

PAGE 60

cake   kite   cube
bone   hive   robe
slide   flute   plate
globe **plane** **crane**

PAGE 61

15 + 2 = **17**   7 + **10** = 17
5 + 6 = **11**   2 + **9** = **11**
13 + 3 = **16**   8 + **8** = **16**
18   10
13   19
14   20

PAGE 62

Answers will vary. Some possible answers are shown below.

lion   fire engine   kids
zookeeper   siren   swings
monkey   safety   trees

round	fast	colorful
button	car	balloons
wheel	cheetah	paintings
fluffy	**mushy**	**brave**
pillow	oatmeal	leader
bunny	peaches	kid

PAGE 63

5 friends
lion
7 friends
2 more friends

PAGE 64

? — green star
. — blue star
! — purple star
. or ! — yellow star
? — green star
. or ! — yellow star
. — blue star
! — purple star

PAGE 65

Answers will vary.

PAGE 66

amphibians
They eat bugs.

Answers will vary. Some possible answers are shown below.

Frogs	Toads
• jump far and fast	• hop and walk
• smooth skin	• bumpy skin
• long legs	• short legs

Answer key

PAGE 67

4	1	3	2
2	3	1	4
3	2	4	1
1	4	2	3

2	4	3	1
1	3	4	2
3	1	2	4
4	2	1	3

1	4	3	2
3	2	1	4
4	1	2	3
2	3	4	1

1	2	4	3
4	3	2	1
2	1	3	4
3	4	1	2

PAGE 68

Drawings will vary.

PAGE 71

tie	seal	goal
mail	boat	blue
deer	bean	train

PAGE 72

north
west
south
east
west

PAGE 73

quiet
playful
sleepy
excited

PAGE 74

4 tens + 3 ones = 43
8 tens + 5 ones = 85
6 tens + 7 ones = 67

2 tens + 6 ones = 26   5 tens + 8 ones = 58
3 tens + 7 ones = 37   6 tens + 2 ones = 62
9 tens + 0 ones = 90   7 tens + 4 ones = 74

PAGE 75

down — up
friendly — kind
near — far
after — before
close — shut
slow — fast
save — keep
never — always
behind — ahead
tell — ask
few — many
gentle — soft

PAGE 76

 3 tens + 6 ones = 36

 5 tens + 2 ones = 52

 2 tens + 9 ones = 29

 7 tens + 0 ones = 70

 4 tens + 7 ones = 47

PAGE 77

near
above
beside
between
on
under
behind

PAGE 78

4 tens + 5 ones = 45
8 tens + 2 ones = 82
3 tens + 8 ones = 38
6 tens + 3 ones = 63
9 tens + 9 ones = 99
8 tens + 0 ones = 80
2 tens + 7 ones = 27

PAGE 79

A COLD
AN EGG
A COIN
A TOWEL
LIGHT
STAIRS
YOUR AGE

PAGE 80

	Camp activity			
	Soccer	Swimming	Crafts	Sailing
Lisa	X	X	X	●
Xavier	X	X	●	X
Jade	X	●	X	X
Eric	●	X	X	X

sailing
crafts
swimming
soccer

PAGE 81

25 < 48   83 > 68
87 < 92   51 = 51
24 < 41   54 > 48
21 > 19   62 < 71
74 > 47   38 > 37

26   43   58
74   87   93
58   60   67
24   28   30   34
16   46   60   64
83   88   92   96

PAGE 82

Answer key

PAGE 83

living	living	nonliving
living	nonliving	living
nonliving	nonliving	living

PAGE 84

Sample answer: It rained for three weeks.

The sun is shining.

Sample answer: flower seeds

PAGE 85

Feelings	Jobs
• sad • joyful • upset	• nurse • teacher • pilot
Things you wear	**Snacks for a picnic**
• pants • shirt • dress	• cookies • grapes • popcorn

Answers will vary. Some possible answers are shown below.

Body parts	Things that fly

PAGE 86

28	19
47	34
59	26
68	19
37	46
78	98

PAGE 87

future tense

past tense

present tense

past tense

past tense

present tense

future tense

Answers will vary.

PAGE 88

27 + 6 = 33

35 + 9 = 44

18 + 7 = 25

42 + 8 = 50

41	92
24	31
62	53
83	70
32	65

PAGE 89

☀ = 16   ⛱ = 7   🍦 = 20

🐢 = 10   🕶 = 6   ⭐ = 13

PAGE 90

⚙	🍗	🍉	📋	🐚	👒	🍦	📷	🗡	⭐
9	8	4	6	9	5	4	7	5	6

PAGE 91

The penguins swim, play, and hunt for food in the gentle waves.

large rocks

Answers will vary. Some possible answers are shown below.

1. Penguins hunt in the calm water.
2. The boulders hide the penguins' nests.

PAGE 92

57	49	68
23	59	27
38	37	83

28	54	19
+31	+44	+60
59	98	79

45	33	82
+22	+41	+14
67	74	96

PAGE 93

START	brave	fell	flip	ant
nick	heal	blob	crust	bus
home	mice	moss	went	help
tube	cling	just	doll	lock
wait	pay	scene	queen	tried
lunch	bump	hand	dust	coal
truck	milk	smell	true	eve
loss	space	low	sweet	print
hill	twice	fix	chest	dash
dusk	green	age	blue	FINISH

PAGE 94

62	71	34
50	35	61
43	51	90

38	64	29
+25	+17	+41
63	81	70

26	54	37
+69	+18	+47
95	72	84

PAGE 95

Amir sees a (big) crab.

I counted (eleven) shells.

My (clean) clothes are in the bag.

The kite has a (long) string.

The (tall) waves crash on the beach.

Jess ran on the (yellow) sand.

Owen gets (two) shovels for the bucket.

Answers will vary. Some possible answers are below.

| cold | shiny | red |
| sweet | long | two |

PAGE 96

| stream | waterfall | river |
| lake | ocean | bay |

PAGE 97

Tom feels sleepy.

She loves pizza.

Alvin plants a tree.

Emily made a snack.

Answer key

PAGE 97 *(continued)*

Calves are baby cows.

We ran around the park.

The baker made ten cakes.

The rain fell all day long.

PAGE 98

53 + 6 = 59	17 + 24 = 41	45 + 31 = 76	81 + 3 = 84	13 + 35 = 48	36 + 24 = 60
23 + 57 = 80	67 + 9 = 76	82 + 6 = 88	45 + 27 = 72	39 + 9 = 48	34 + 12 = 46
18 + 58 = 76	51 + 45 = 96	64 + 19 = 83	23 + 26 = 49	26 + 22 = 48	63 + 8 = 71

12 + 35 = 47	37 + 26 = 63	65 + 9 = 74	38 + 27 = 65	13 + 42 = 55	54 + 6 = 60
74 + 6 = 80	53 + 4 = 57	11 + 46 = 57	67 + 13 = 80	56 + 9 = 65	45 + 21 = 66
58 + 35 = 93	88 + 5 = 93	49 + 44 = 93	70 + 16 = 86	37 + 44 = 81	61 + 4 = 65

PAGE 99

Answers will vary.

PAGE 100

CITY
MILK
SHAPE
PAPER
HONEY
BASKET

PAGE 103

19 dogs

21 holes

60 cupcakes

51 times

67 pictures

PAGE 104

a minute

a dog

a mountain

the start

shouting

day   week   year
pond   lake   ocean
child parent grandma

PAGE 105

4:00   9:00   2:30
7:00   11:30   5:30

PAGE 106

Sample answer: Jamie feels shy about his voice.

It is easier to face something new with someone else.

PAGE 107

54 − 3 = 51   28 − 5 = 23

86 − 2 = 84   39 − 6 = 33

11   82
53   73
62   20
42   91

PAGE 108

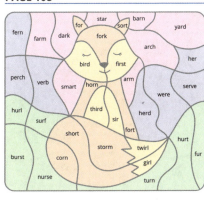

PAGE 109

```
  F R U I T
      O
  S F L O W E R S
  E   T       T
  L E A V E S  E
  D           M
  S
```

PAGE 109 *(continued)*

Across	Down
1. FRUIT	2. ROOTS
4. FLOWERS	3. SEEDS
6. LEAVES	5. STEM

PAGE 110

watched

closed

surprised

walked

landed

painted

guessed

smelled

packed

tasted

PAGE 111

Answers will vary.

PAGE 112

5	8	1
6	2	4
3	7	9

14 17 14

9	2	5
3	1	4
6	7	8

18 10 17

7	4	5
1	9	2
6	8	3

14 21 10

8	2	6
4	7	3
1	9	5

13 18 14

1	8	3
6	7	4
2	9	5

9 24 12

9	6	4
3	1	7
5	8	2

17 15 13

14 12 16
19 8
19 21

16
14
15

12
17
16

19
11
15

PAGE 113

ABC order

a dictionary

a meerkat that watches out for danger

Sample answer: in a burrow

PAGE 114

43 − 20 = 23   27 − 10 = 17

Answer key

PAGE 114 *(continued)*

85 − 50 = 35   79 − 70 = 9

32   16
24   8
11   20
5   27

PAGE 115

2   1   2   3   3   1

START
after	funny	going	help	long
please	small	began	bumpy	click
bring	cry	land	garden	night
without	summer	penny	number	place
broken	chase	edge	kept	proud
FINISH

PAGE 116

service   good   service
service   service   good
good   service   good

PAGE 117

picked
excited
large
tired
build

Answers will vary. Some possible answers are shown below.

fast
love
tall

PAGE 118

14   33   63
60   14   51
26   91   20

79   37   64
− 5   − 6   − 30
74   31   34

23   95   45
− 20   − 70   − 2
3   25   43

PAGE 119

We watched (the) huge whales from (a) boat.

When I bring (a) cake into (the) room, we will yell, "Surprise!"

Jill likes to dip (an) apple in peanut butter for (a) snack.

She made (an) octopus and (a) seahorse out of balloons.

Next summer, we'll use (the) rope swing to jump in (the) water.

a
an
a
a
an

PAGE 120

12 toys
33 colored pencils
36 strawberries
55 stickers
24 balloons

PAGE 121

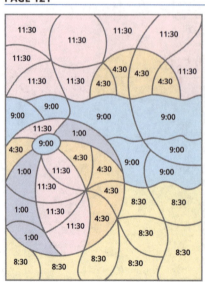

PAGE 122

~~band~~	ape	ham	sing	hill	~~dig~~
rack	~~grand~~	bash	sink	king	~~pig~~
aid	clay	~~hand~~	this	bring	~~big~~

bear	care	please	show	~~down~~	cow
eat	heard	there	how	~~brown~~	grow
~~dear~~	~~near~~	~~year~~	know	~~town~~	now

PAGE 122 *(continued)*

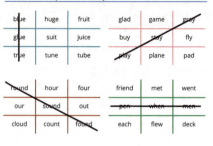

PAGE 123

The whistle is 2 inches long.
The s'more is 3 inches long.
The craft stick is 5 inches long.
The bracelet is 6 inches long.

4 inches longer

8 inches

PAGE 124

What
When
Where
Who
Why

Answers will vary. Some possible answers are shown below.

What did you do yesterday?
When did you eat lunch?
Why do birds sing?
Where is your house?

PAGE 125

```
  61       14       32       87       68       36
− 10     + 27     + 29     − 30     +  7     + 22
  51       41       61       57       75       58

  56       49       21       47       14       95
−  6     −  8     + 40     −  4     + 43     − 50
  50       41       61       43       57       45

  19       11       64       16       17       59
+ 43     + 30     − 30     +  5     − 10     −  2
  62       41       34       21        7       57

  49       19       62       39       83       59
− 30     + 51     +  6     −  9     − 50     +  1
  19       70       68       30       33       60

  86       35       76       64       27       45
− 40     + 27     −  6     + 11     + 33     −  2
  46       62       70       75       60       43

  33       58       67       80       48       51
+ 30     +  5     −  4     − 20     + 33     +  4
  63       63       63       60       81       55
```

140   © IXL Learning

Answer key

PAGE 126

nighttime

Answers will vary. Some possible answers are shown below.
owls, bats, foxes, crickets, wolves

crickets, wolves

Answers will vary. Some possible answers are shown below.
away/play or wings/sing or prowl/howl

PAGE 127

75 balloons

8 kids

19 seconds longer

31 hot dogs

20 ice pops

PAGE 128

cupcake

doorbell

rainbow

catfish

butterfly

basketball

PAGE 128 *(continued)*

flash | light

foot | ball

lady | bug

pop | corn

dog | house

PAGE 129

amphibian   reptile   bird

mammal   fish   amphibian

PAGE 130

sell

We

makes

You

want

He

sing

I

looks

They

PAGE 130 *(continued)*

He

She

We

I

PAGE 131

		Lunchbox color			
		Yellow	Green	Pink	Orange
Snack	Hummus	●	X	X	X
	Pretzels	X	X	●	X
	Orange	X	X	X	●
	Crackers	X	●	X	X

yellow

pink

orange

green

PAGE 132

Answers will vary.

© IXL Learning

Notes

Certificate of Completion

Congratulations!

_____
Name

has completed this year's
Ultimate Summer Workbook
and is ready for grade 2!

_____
Date

Awarded by